DAVID M. LENZ

Urban *and* Rural Paintings *of* Wisconsin

1 *Tugboat*, 1998 Oil on board, 11 1/4 x 18 in.

Interview by: *Jeffrey R. Hayes*

Social commentary essays by:
Daniel J. Bader, Tanya Cromartie-Twaddle, Coretta Herring, Secretary Rod Nilsestuen,
Richard R. Pieper Sr. and Martin F. Stein

Poems by:
Tiara Cannon, Marlisa Harris and Carlton Young

Book and article excerpts by:
Ben Logan and Crocker Stephenson

CHARLES
ALLIS
ART
MUSEUM

ACKNOWLEDGMENTS

We are grateful to the following sponsors for making this book possible.

Special thanks to:
Daniel and Linda Bader
Mr. and Mrs. Leslie Muma
TECHSTAFF INC

Additional support was provided by:

Steve and Jane Chernof
Mr. and Mrs. George Dalton
Mr. and Mrs. John F. Monroe Jr.
Payne & Dolan Inc.
Pieper Electric Inc.

Barbara Stein
Marty Stein
Mr. and Mrs. Thomas R. Tuschen
West Bend Mutual Insurance Co.

Editing: Tom Tolan
Graphic Design: Dave Paulmann
Photography: Robert Melkonian, Nsync Studio
Printing: Burton & Mayer Inc.

David would like to recognize Richard and Sue Pieper for their continued and unwavering support.

And finally, David would like to dedicate this book to Rosemarie and Sam.

This catalog is published on the occasion of the exhibition
David M. Lenz: Urban and Rural Paintings of Wisconsin organized and presented by the Charles Allis Art Museum from September 29 to October 31, 2004.

Published by Past Press, 3118 N. Pierce Street, Milwaukee, WI 53212 in cooperation with the Charles Allis Art Museum, 1801 N. Prospect Avenue, Milwaukee, WI 53202.

©2004 Charles Allis Art Museum. All rights reserved.

Library of Congress Control Number: 2004111868

ISBN 0-9703613-4-3

Profits from the sale of this book will go to the Boys & Girls Clubs of Greater Milwaukee.

CONTENTS

24 *Looking Back, (Detail)* 1995
Oil on linen, 44 x 54 in.

INTRODUCTION

Have you ever flipped through a family photo album and been struck by images of relatives you didn't even know? Something in their faces revealed an inner strength, dignity or joy that leapt off of the page. That is the experience I had while viewing the remarkable work of David M. Lenz. Lenz captures the humanity, and humility, of our extended human family and then invites us into a dialogue that binds viewer, artist and subject.

This catalogue is an extension of that conversation. In addition to presenting his paintings – and discussions about them – Lenz has invited people who are passionate about the worlds his work depicts to offer their views in essays, poems and excerpts from longer writings. It is his hope that this catalogue will spark ideas and discussions about the many issues facing all of us as we investigate our connections to our surroundings and to each other.

The Charles Allis Art Museum is proud to host this important exhibition, which runs from September 29 through October 31, 2004. This is Lenz's first solo mid-career retrospective. Nearly half the works in this exhibition, including several major pieces, are on public display for the first time. It would be nearly impossible to undertake an exhibition such as this without help. We are fortunate that a community of supporters has emerged to assist in the creation of the exhibition and this catalogue including:

• A dozen Milwaukee area art collectors and businesses who sponsored this catalogue

• 27 individuals and businesses who loaned paintings for the exhibition

• Linda and Daniel Bader for their especially generous support

• University of Wisconsin-Milwaukee Art History Professor Jeffrey R. Hayes for his perceptive interview

• Careful and thoughtful editing by Tom Tolan

• Beautiful graphic design by David Paulmann

• The staff of the Charles Allis Art Museum, especially Manager of Exhibitions and Collections Sarah Haberstroh Stauder

• The 12 writers and essayists who took time to contribute to the catalogue

I have had the wonderful experiences of leading cultural institutions in vibrant urban settings and directing a historic site in an agricultural community of 500 people. I feel that I have looked at the same people that David Lenz has painted, but until now I may have never really seen them.

James D. Temmer
Executive Director
Charles Allis/Villa Terrace Art Museums

39 *Thistles (Detail)*, 2001
Oil on linen, 32 x 54 in.

PAINTING THE UNSUNG
An Interview with David M. Lenz

Jeffrey R. Hayes
Professor of Art History, University of Wisconsin-Milwaukee

Jeffrey Hayes: David, when did you become serious about painting?

David Lenz: From childhood, really. My grandfather was a painter. He made copies of European masters' work. He had a large batch of prints of all types of artists, and customers would come to his studio and pick out something they liked. They would say, "I'd like a 24-by-30 oil of this," and he would copy it. So, basically, he was a kind of blue-collar painter.

JH: Did your grandfather encourage you to become a painter?

DL: Absolutely. His name was Nic Lenz, and he passed away when I was about fourteen years old, so he didn't really get the chance to see me develop, but I can distinctly remember sitting on his knee and showing him my paintings and him saying: "Remember, the trees have to look like a bird could fly into them, but here it looks as if a bird were to fly into your trees, they wouldn't be able to find the branches!" So, that's how it started.

JH: Beyond your grandfather, who else has shaped your direction as artist?

DL: Tom Uttech [former Professor of Painting, University of Wisconsin-Milwaukee] was the most influential. I went to Canada two times with him in a summer course that he called Canadian Canoe Workshop. That was a wonderful experience, because on a two-week trip I did twelve to fourteen paintings on location. He would do critiques with me right there sitting on the rocks in front of a lake.

JH: What sort of critical feedback did you get—do you remember anything specific that planted the seeds for your own particular development?

DL: There was a lot of discussion about what was out there in reality versus what I was including in my paintings, and I remember him saying over and over again, "Just because it's out there doesn't mean it has to land in your painting." I also remember him giving me valuable pointers on color, because I wasn't yet using color the way I wanted to. And just his example – I recall going to see an exhibition of his at Dorothy Bradley Gallery back when she was on Downer Avenue. I was taking a course with him at the time, and I was blown away by the show. The way he handles paint had a big influence on me as well. He often paints in a very transparent manner and lets a lot of what is underneath show through, and I fell in love with that way of painting through seeing his work.

JH: When did you study at UWM?

DL: 1980 to 1985.

JH: And you earned a BFA?

DL: Yes, a Bachelor of Fine Arts in visual communications. I wasn't a Fine Arts major; I was a graphic designer.

JH: Why didn't you major in painting?

DL: Because I thought it was a much more practical way to go. I had watched my grandfather struggle to make a living. The life of an artist isn't the easiest life, and I thought graphic design would be a way for me to make a decent living and still use my abilities as an artist. It was a compromise, and after I graduated I got a job right away with a publishing company and then moved on to become art director for an advertising agency. There I was, about twenty-seven years old, already with some success in my career and even a little money saved because I was living cheaply. At that point, I thought that I could buy a house and continue with my work as an art director, or I could use that money to finance a year's sabbatical from advertising and try painting full-time. Well, my income during that first year as an artist was very low—in fact, I didn't pay any taxes at all because I was living beneath the poverty level—but then I entered my first Lakefront Festival of the Arts, began to develop a following, and I haven't looked back since.

JH: One more background question. Who would you say have been your art historical models—do you see yourself in relation to the history of art in any particular ways?

3 *Batchewaung Bay, Quetico Provincial Park,* 1984
Oil on board, 14 x 11 in.

4 *Ballard Lake, Wisconsin,* 1985
Oil on board, 14 x 11 in.

DL: I admire the nineteenth-century Hudson River painters—Thomas Cole, and especially Frederic Church. Church's ability to paint on location was without peer. He could paint so quickly and was wonderfully adept at capturing what he saw. I looked at his paintings a lot when I was in college. The next historical group that I gravitated toward was Ashcan School artists such as John Sloan and George Bellows. And also the Regionalists, Grant Wood especially. There is something about his very carefully designed paintings and the repetition of different shapes throughout his compositions that I find appealing, as well as his surfaces, which I think are quite beautiful.

JH: Any more recent sources or influences?

DL: As far as contemporaries, for a long time I didn't look at the art magazines at all, because I felt really disconnected from modern art. I've always admired artists who have gone through their careers with blinders on, who have done their own thing no matter what other artists in the world are doing,

5 *Bud-Fern Falls, Quetico Provincial Park,* 1984
Oil on board, 11 x 14 in.

artists such as Georgia O'Keeffe, Winslow Homer and Thomas Eakins. In the case of O'Keeffe, whose career spanned Cubism and Abstract Expressionism, she kept to her own vision of what mattered and painted in her own way. That's what I admire, and so I almost *don't* want to know what else is going on. However, I have noticed quite a bit of realism recently, which is encouraging to me, since when I was a student and for a long time afterward, realism was dead.

JH: Your particular regard for Frederic Church struck a chord with me, mainly in terms of light. That's where I see a strong connection with your paintings.

DL: Yes, how light strikes things, how light reacts, how it affects the way we look at the world—those are all things that fascinate me.

JH: My sense is that the light in your paintings does not just function physically. For artists of Church's generation, of course, light often served as a metaphor for the divine or spiritual in the world. I'm not suggesting you are exactly the same, but it seems to me that there are strong similarities.

DL: Yes, I agree, and to some extent I would even say that I do share Church's vision of light as a divine metaphor. In fact, there is this painting by Sanford Gifford, Church's contemporary, I can't remember the title, but it's in the Metropolitan Museum of Art…

JH: *Kauterskill Clove?*

DL: You know the painting! It's wonderful. It has this luminous, all-encompassing golden light. Recently, I finished a painting that has a sun ball like that in a very warm color, and since I sometimes give paintings a temporary working title, I called that one the Gifford painting.

JH: Here's more of an academic question. Painting has been called moribund or worse by a number of recent critics and even some artists. It has been judged irrelevant in the postmodern world, and marked as elitist, formalistic, a mere commodity and so forth. How do you react to that?

6 *From Trail Ridge Road, Rocky Mountain National Park,* 1996
Watercolor on paper, 5 ³/₄ x 8 ³/₄ in.

DL: I guess that's why I never read the art journals! I think it's pretty silly talk, to be honest with you. It's like when television came along; people said movies would die, yet movies are bigger than ever. And you can go through so many other things in modern life that were marked as certain to change or go away, but I don't think painting will ever go away. I think it's a form of expression like letter writing. People said that with email, letters would disappear, but they haven't; it's going to change, and maybe it won't be as prevalent as it once was, but it's never going to go away completely. And I think painting is the same. There are certain forms of expression that are so interesting and rich and basic to the ways human beings express themselves that I don't think they are ever going to disappear, and I believe painting is one of those.

JH: You also uphold the claim that your paintings are "journalistic," which I believe derives from one of [Milwaukee Journal Sentinel] critic James Auer's earlier reviews of your work. Many painters would run from that particular descriptor—why are you accepting, even approving of it?

DL: Indeed, among the key influences on my painting that I cited before, I should have included photojournalism. There is an immediacy and authenticity to good photojournalism that is very powerful. I look at such photographs and see a visual language that I like, a language that captures a slice of reality in unique ways.

JH: Any specific examples come to mind?

DL: No, but when I paint I try to represent things authentically like a journalist. If I change aspects of a scene, which I often do, the color of a coat for example, it must all still end up absolutely plausible. I want everything to be visually comfortable so that when it's viewed it feels like a slice of reality, so that you're almost standing in the snow with that boy on the street [alluding to his 2004 oil *The Familiar Path*]. If I can recreate that street in a completely plausible way, so you feel you can almost walk into the painting, then maybe you can stand there and relate to the boy and his life and have a sense of what it would be like to walk a mile in his shoes. If I can do that, I think I'm taking a slice of reality, putting a frame around it, shining a spotlight on it, and enticing people to look—to look at parts of reality that they sometimes don't care to see.

JH: This reminds me of the debate surrounding some Depression-era documentary photography, such as Dorothea Lange's famous *Migrant Mother*. Some people feel that because this photograph was set up and not entirely spontaneous that it falls short of the truth. Others say that a photograph or other image doesn't have to be accurate in a literal way to capture the truth of a condition or historical moment; in fact, sometimes you need to synthesize or reconstitute a variety of evidence in order to capture a higher truth or a fuller sense of the reality you are trying to represent through art.

DL: The latter viewpoint is essentially what I'm trying to do. No, you can't manipulate everything, but if you have the goal of being truthful and accurate in mind, it doesn't matter if that chain link fence was exactly where I've painted it or five feet away—it's still part of the neighborhood and part of the reality of that boy's life. So, I don't view little manipulations like that, of the right type, as dishonest.

JH: Why change anything at all then?

DL: It's a visual matter. In addition to capturing a meaningful slice of reality, I'm trying to make a visually interesting painting. I want the painting to be honest, but at the same time I want it to function as an interesting piece of art. So the composition, the color arrangement, that's all very important as well, and those considerations are always in the back of my mind.

JH: Do you see any conflict between your aesthetic standards—standards of what might be called artistic quality—and the social or moral responsibilities you also embrace as an artist? On your web site, for example, you speak more of "hope" than beauty when discussing the value or impact of your paintings. I've also noticed that your work is often used to support community service programs, especially for children. Is there ever any tension between your pictorial standards and your content-based social concerns?

DL: The challenge of achieving a balance between such goals is always a difficult one. How do you find that balance? That's a good question. I think it's a basic human quality to want to be hopeful about the future of society…. I want my paintings to have a very strong sense of reality, including the things that aren't so good about a neighborhood, but I also want them to reflect my need to be hopeful that things can get better…. To answer your question another way, back in college I began to focus on landscape, and although I now know that landscape paintings can carry social and political meaning, at that point I was just trying to capture a scene or a creek or a certain kind of light in a limited amount of time.

38 *The Familiar Path*, 2004
Oil on linen, 28 x 34 in.

Basically, I was honing my *technical* skills as a painter. It was a great exercise, but eventually I realized I couldn't continue with that as my life's work—simply finding and painting visually beautiful landscapes.

JH: So what happened to make you go past that?

DL: If there was ever a eureka moment for me as an artist it came when I put my first child into a painting. My first large painting that included a child—it's called *Riverwest* and now belongs to Northwestern Mutual—was of a boy getting ready to sled down a hill. As soon as I drew it out—I did a charcoal first—I knew that I had found my life's work. I read the newspaper every day and the problems of the city really get to me. I feel for the kids growing up in many central Milwaukee neighborhoods; they have a tough time of it. And I compare it to my own childhood—I grew up in Brookfield and was pretty sheltered… Some people won't even drive through the inner city. But these kids call it their home. They play there, live there, go to school there, and everyone knows about the city's struggling public school system. These kinds of problems really stick in the back of my mind, and I know a lot of other socially conscious people, people who buy my paintings, who are bothered, too, and are trying to make things better. If nothing else, then, as a painter I can take a slice of what's going on in the city and stick it on a museum or gallery wall where others will hopefully see and think about it.

JH: Along the same lines, it's amazing to me that people are sometimes surprised by questions that seek to make connections between artists and society. Even some artists are uncomfortable with questions like that, but we seldom dismiss such a proposition when we're talking about a nurse or teacher or lawyer or almost any other professional.

DL: How boring it would be to live in a world where things were made just to look nice, where art didn't have any real meaning or point of view …

JH: And yet there are those who would insist that you're still operating from a rather privileged position, that you may be painting inner city kids, but how involved are you really in making change? What kind of real impact do you have when you make paintings that are purchased mostly by rich collectors?

DL: Well, of course I'm an artist, not a political leader or a social worker, though I am trying to use what I do – paint pictures – to in some small way effect positive change. I believe that in order to make society better, it's going to take *everybody*. No question that when I labor over a painting for several months, I must ask a

relatively high price in order to make a living. It can't be a $500 painting if I've spent three months on it. So, inevitably, most of my paintings end up on the walls of affluent, though not always exceptionally wealthy, people. I feel deeply indebted to my patrons because without their support these paintings would not exist at all. No artist can survive without patrons. But I also really enjoy it when the general public can see my work. Next month I'm going to hang some prints of my work in my neighborhood barbershop. Three years ago I did a giant painting of five children who were treated at Children's Hospital of Wisconsin. The painting hangs in the lobby of the hospital and a couple hundred thousand people walk by it every year. People from all walks of life. And the last time I showed my big farm scene *Thistles* at the Charles Allis, a husband and wife, dairy farmers, drove down from Sheboygan just to attend the opening. That really meant a lot to me. As for my being "privileged," I don't think you'd say that if you saw my tax return. It is very difficult to make a living as an artist.

JH: Do you have any continuing awareness of the lives or circumstances of your subjects, the city kids you paint for example, or do you just photograph them and go on with your life? Any kind of ongoing connection?

DL: That's a tough question. In some ways I would like there to be an ongoing relationship after the painting is finished, but I don't know how possible that is. It seems right now I barely have enough time to spend with my own seven-year-old son. I've always wanted to, for example, volunteer for Big Brothers Big Sisters, and some day I will. In another way, though, if you paint something very specific—a specific person, place or time—which is kind of what I'm doing, if you capture it well enough, it can become universal, because human experiences are human experiences. So then the idea or image assumes a larger context, and its meaning can be appreciated as universal. I think that's what I'm seeing with the kids a lot of the time.

JH: Since so many of your paintings represent children, are you ever concerned that they might become too sentimental?

DL: That's something I look out for. You know, I never consciously set out to make paintings of children. It just evolved, and I think it evolved because children are the innocent bystanders of society. Wherever they're born and wherever they grow up, it's not of their own choosing. And so I think all the problems of society seem that much more heartbreaking when they affect children. It ratchets up the human emotions.

7 *Sunrise,* 1998
Oil on linen 20 x 24 in.

11

JH: I'm struck by the city/country duality of your subject matter. We've talked mostly about the city side, but there's this rural dimension, too. Is there a symbiotic relationship between these two aspects of your work?

DL: At one point, I was painting city scenes exclusively. I had rented an east side apartment and saved some money, and I thought—wouldn't it be great to have a little getaway. Where I was living there were just sidewalks, no birds, hardly any trees, and buses going by all the time. It was *never* quiet. Even at two in the morning there were usually people arguing outside my apartment. So I bought forty wooded acres in south-central Wisconsin. This was my antidote for city life, being able to just go up there and pitch a tent and listen to the birds. Eventually I got to know my closest neighbors, Erv and Mercedes Wagner, who are dairy farmers. They own a very small farm, only one hundred and twenty acres, about sixty of which are tillable, and even when they were operating at full capacity they

probably never milked more than thirty cows. When I painted them they were milking only about fifteen. Most of all, what intrigued me about the Wagners was their very modest, even humble lifestyle, yet this seemed to matter very little when you were in their company or speaking with them. They live rich lives, they love their life, and I don't think they've ever wished for it to be any different. I admire that quality in people, lacking means but rich in character. And so my painting them was a continuation of painting people we don't always notice or recognize.

JH: You say you paint *people*, and although we've been talking about the city or country as subject, it seems to me that what you really do is paint people who happen to be situated in these two classic environments. Clearly, you wouldn't have been satisfied just to paint your forty acres, to paint pure landscape. You have to have human subjects, unlike your very early works, which didn't include people. I'd like you to talk a little more about that, and also about any connection between your urban and rural subjects, between the city kids and the Wagners.

DL: Again, these are all people whom society doesn't see a lot of the time no matter where they live. These are unsung, ordinary people, yet they are the people I most admire and find interesting. I've been asked many times to do portraits of prominent people; for example, I was once approached about painting each member of a Milwaukee company's board, a $50,000 commission altogether, but there was no way I could do that. It just didn't sit right with me. You can't say directors of large companies are unsung. I would much rather spend my time shining a spotlight on members of our society whom we don't always look at, and so if my subjects have a connection it would be more about that, about the *unsung*.

JH: Actually, I don't think anyone has ever called you a portrait painter, and yet it strikes me that on some essential level that's what you are …

DL: Oh, I think I am, absolutely. Sometimes when I look at my work overall, I say: "There it is, one person standing in front with a background. Boy, am I repeating myself." But that form of having someone close in and looking right back, almost like there is a conversation between subject and viewer—we're looking at them and who they are, but they're also looking back at us and judging who we are and what we're doing—that right-in-your-face confrontation between the viewer and the subject is something that I just keep coming back to and can't get enough of. That's what I'm about as a painter.

JH: And yet you don't title your paintings as portraits *per se*; you don't use proper names that I can recall. Why not? … What's the title of this painting?

8 *Student,* 1993
Oil on board, 9 x 10 in.

9 *Looking South,* 2002
Oil on linen, 12 x 18 in.

13

DL: I call it *No Luck Today*.

JH: Why not simply name the two young fishermen who are centered both formally and emotionally in the painting?

DL: Because, as I said before, it's both a specific portrayal of these boys, but it's also universal in the sense that they represent many other kids. What I'm trying to say with *No Luck Today* is—here are these two young African-Americans posed against the Milwaukee skyline, and all the wealth and power of the city is concentrated downtown, but what does that wealth and power have to do with these kids who live neither downtown nor in the expensive suburbs? In fact,

10 *Portrait of Sam Lenz*, 1999
Oil on board, 6 x 7 in.

I didn't photograph these kids at the harbor at all, but on the grounds of the LaVarnway Boys and Girls Club at 15th and Locust, a very tough neighborhood near where they live.

JH: This painting reminds me that I also wanted to ask you to compare yourself to Edward Hopper, another urban realist …

DL: I like that comparison a lot. I should have mentioned Hopper earlier as a major influence because of the way he placed his people within the context of the city and his keen grasp of human emotions in relation to living in the modern city. And he frequently depicted one figure alone with the city, which is often my own format. I also like that he marched to his own aesthetic while much of the rest of the art world was moving in a completely different direction. Andrew Wyeth is another prime example of that. He was at the height of his powers and the only realist that anyone could think of in the Sixties and Seventies. I admired the way he got to know his subjects, the way he often lived and worked among them. Like Hopper, there is also great emotion in Wyeth's paintings, and capturing emotion is something I'm very interested in.

JH: You usually photograph your subjects before you paint them, although no single photograph ever serves as the prototype for your finished composition. Compare your intensely realistic oil paintings to the current vogue for large format color photography—ultimately, what are some essential differences?

DL: The general public views photography as the cool, objective capturing of reality. It's exact and mechanical, and no brush is involved. Clearly, though, photography doesn't simply replicate reality. There are so many things that photography distorts and changes; it flattens space, for example. And that's where I come in as a painter. Over the course of weeks or months working on a painting, carefully considering every aspect, agonizing over the placement and color of each element, hopefully I will add a level of richness to the scene, both visually and emotionally, that will make it better than anything I can photograph. I've never taken a photograph that I felt should be enlarged and hung on a wall. I've never made a photograph that good. If I had that ability, I might do it, but I don't. I'm a painter and I use photography as a tool.

JH: Just to finish here, any significant shifts or new ideas on the horizon?

DL: I want to get back to painting more city scenes with kids, and because I have a son with special needs, I plan to do some paintings of people with disabilities. That will be an important new direction for me.

11 *No Luck Today,* 1995
Oil on linen, 26 x 36 in.

12 *North Avenue,* 1990
Oil on linen, 14 ¼ x 20 in.

13 *Seated Boy,* 1992
Oil on board, 9 x 10 in.

14 *New Faces,* 1992
Oil on board, 9 x 10 in.

16

15 *Newhall Street,* 1992
Oil on linen, 26 x 32 in.

HEALING THE WORLD
THE AMERICAN TRADITION OF DOING GOOD

By Martin F. Stein

America is a fledgling in world history, yet we wear our rich heritage like a badge and are compelled to share its brilliance with the rest of mankind. Democracy and freedom are the cornerstones of our great nation, but we are not the sole exchequers of liberty's endless treasures. What is unique about America is the character of Americans. Alexis de Tocqueville identified our national character following his visit to our country in 1831. In his classic book, *Democracy in America,* he observed: "I must say that I have often seen Americans make great and real sacrifices to the public welfare; and I have noticed a hundred instances in which they hardly ever failed to lend faithful support to one another." What de Tocqueville discovered is that Americans care and are willing to do something to right a wrong or effect a change that might make life easier or better or more just for someone else.

The spirit of caring and willingness to act underlies the origins of philanthropy in American society. Some of our largest and best national organizations were founded by persistent individuals, who were moved to act to correct social injustices, reduce the miseries of the impoverished or make new immigrants feel welcome on freedom's strange shores.

Big Brothers (today Big Brothers Big Sisters) was founded in New York City in 1904 by Ernest Coulter, a clerk in the juvenile court, who recognized the need for young people to have a mentor in their lives. The Boys Club (now Boys & Girls Clubs of America) was founded in 1860 in Hartford, Conn., by a group of women who were concerned about the safety and welfare of young boys they observed roaming the streets. In 1887, five clergymen and a woman who headed a social service agency created a community-wide charitable campaign in Denver.

16 *The Black Door,* 1993
Oil on board, 9 x 10 in.

Their goal was to address the problem of miners who sought wealth and fortune in Colorado, but instead became impoverished and died, or returned to their homes, leaving their children behind as orphans without community programs to serve them. That campaign evolved over the years into what is now the United Way of America.

By acting on the problems they observed and inspiring others to take action, these individuals of conscience had the power to harness the collective character of Americans to resolve social concerns and bring relief to suffering.

That the world has changed is undeniable, but the progress of the world has only transformed the nature of our problems. More than ever, Americans as individuals and Americans as a collective force for change must give their time and their resources to support organizations that nurture social healing. Americans today must retain the same character and the same compassion as Americans of the past, who were inspired to work together to resolve the ills of their times.

America does not have the exclusive on philanthropy, but no country in the world does it better. Why? Because we prize our freedom and cherish the rights and protections afforded by democratic ideals. Because we are seekers of justice and fairness and the human rights of all peoples of the world. Because we refuse to allow fear and uncertainty to cloud our vision of what needs to be done, nor our willingness to do it.

Americans are indeed a people of action, and this is the badge of brilliance we strive to share with all nations of the world. Every individual in America has the right, the power and, yes, the obligation, to stand up and *act* to make a difference. Above all, this is our most sacred American freedom.

There is a concept in Jewish religious thought called *tikun olam*, which means to repair or heal the world. The writer Eugene Morgulis discusses it in a way that speaks to the generosity of Americans: "To heal the world, we must first see what is wrong," he writes. "The things that we would rather turn away from, it is those things which we must correct. Although we may wonder, 'What can I do? I am but one person,' all it takes is for one person to stand up and say, 'This is wrong! We must change this!' When the others agree, you will not be one person. You will be an enormous crowd."

17 *Hang Tough*, 1991
Oil on linen, 36 x 42 1/2 in.

18 *Before the Fireworks,* 1993
Oil on linen, 66 x 144 in.

DIVERSE MILWAUKEE

By Daniel J. Bader

My first genuine exposure to Milwaukee's wealth of diversity was in 1976, when at the age of 14 I entered Riverside High School as an incoming freshman. Until that point, I had limited exposure to people different from me. I grew up on the east side of Milwaukee in an upper-middle-class neighborhood, which at that point in the '60s and '70s was entirely white. I attended Jewish schools from pre-school through eighth grade. My exposure to different cultures up until public high school amounted to the occasional black or Native American domestic worker at home, school or synagogue.

My four years at Riverside High school opened my eyes to cultural diversity. Riverside's population in the mid-'70s was composed of about 50% white students and 50% black students. The school did have some racial division, of course, but generally Riverside was a wonderful mixing point for Milwaukee's east side and north side students. There were meaningful interactions in the classrooms, lunchroom and gym among students of all backgrounds. Students from both sides of the Milwaukee River learned from each other and about each other in an intellectually stimulating environment.

Milwaukee draws strength as a city from its population's diversity. From the very poor to the very wealthy, from liberals to conservatives, from blacks to whites, from Hispanics to Hmong, from the south side to the north side, from the Jewish community to the Italian community, Milwaukee is a cultural corner of America. The only problem is that we as a community have not figured out how to embrace our diversity and celebrate our unity. Milwaukee is a community that is hung up on polarization. For some reason, we absolutely insist on focusing on our differences and not our similarities. We insist on living separate cultural lives, when we would be stronger as a community if we came together as one diverse, unified society.

To be sure, there are loads of superb diverse interactions in Milwaukee every day. As president of the Helen Bader Foundation, I have had the great opportunity to observe and interact with many groups. We have great pockets of diversity and cultural harmony tucked into our neighborhoods. Much of that cultural harmony is reflected in our non-profit organizations, with concerned citizens coming together around common themes that transcend race and economic boundaries.

Come visit St. Ann's Center for Intergenerational Care on Milwaukee's south side where you have daily gentle interactions between people of all ages, ethnic origins and economic ability. Here you will find people from vastly different backgrounds who care for each other and are united around improving their mutual well-being. At the Alano Foundation Club on Prospect Ave. on the east side, you will also find people of all backgrounds coming together for the common purpose of recovering from alcoholism and drug addiction. At the Alano Club it does not matter what color your skin is, or what your sexual orientation is, or how much money you have. What matters is that everyone is joined in the mutual goal of living a clean, sober and productive life. The focus is not on differences; the focus is on unity.

In every neighborhood in Milwaukee there are non-profits, schools and businesses that provide the catalyst for Milwaukee's citizens to interact in meaningful ways. The vehicles for interaction exist in Milwaukee as they exist in many cities in America. Unfortunately, we have constructed barriers in our community to keep us apart. Some of the barriers are physical, some political, but by and large, we are mostly constrained by bias and psychological deterrents. We as a community have allowed ourselves to lapse into the more comfortable habit of distancing and isolating ourselves from others just because they are different. We are victims of a misguided collective notion, a "group think," if you will, which is not only shamelessly antiquated, but also wrong and harmful.

In 1976, I awoke one morning and walked into Riverside High School to discover a rich world that had eluded me for 14 years. Just as my understanding of Milwaukee's cultural diversity was enlarged, we as Milwaukeeans also need to enlarge our cultural understanding and embrace our cultural diversity. Our future as a community is bright and strong if we move forward as one collective body, and not as individual parts.

David Lenz has taken it upon himself to creatively reflect the goodness and diversity of Milwaukee and Wisconsin in his paintings. David is not only a superb artist, but he is also committed to highlighting the many cultures within Milwaukee and Wisconsin. He is to be congratulated in his efforts to bring us together as a community so that we may embrace our diversity and celebrate our unity.

19 *Milwaukee's Hope,* 1992
Oil on linen, 40 x 54 in.

DAVID M. LENZ

21 *Snowy Day*, 1993
Oil on linen, 20 x 22 in.

20 *Peace in Our Neighborhood II*, 1993
Oil on linen, 19 x 22 in.

25

Where I'm From
By Tiara Cannon

I'm from 24th Place
where my mother died
when I was 6 years.
Every one misses her, even me.

Where I'm from
the neighborhood is very
bad, a lot of fighting,
swearing and shooting.

Where I'm from
our family goes to
church a lot every Sunday.

Where I'm from
my two brothers have
no idea where their
father is, but I do.
He says he thinks about
me all the time.

Where I'm from
people in my family sing
a lot.

Where I'm from
I think it could be better
where I'm from.

Where I'm from
blacks are killed every day.

I'm from
African-Americans.

Where I'm from
we get soul food.

That's where I'm from.

Where I'm From
By Carlton Young

I'm from a street
where a car can roll over the ground.
I'm from a neighborhood
where cats chase dogs,
where dogs are gone like fog,
where I can look up
at the sky-blue sky
and think about what I hear and see.

I am from a home of six kids
and one independent auntie,
who can't take care of all six of us.
I am from sky-blue sky
and do-do brown dirt,
rugged black streets
with banana-yellow lines.

I am from a good
house.

These three poems are reprinted
from Truth Is, I Remember,
Woodland Pattern Book Center
Poetry Camp 2004, Student Anthology.

Used with permission.

Romel Pearl
By Marlisa Harris

*What I really want to say is I'm thankful
for being here. What I really want to say
is I'm kinda glad for being here today. What
I really want to say is I wish some of
the violence and crime would stop. What I
really want to say is I hope one
day I can achieve my dreams. What I
want to say is I wish that I can be
young again. What I want to say is
I wish my cousin didn't get shot in the
head over nothin'. What I want to say
is I love and care about everybody, even
the people I don't like. What I
want to say is I wish that people
would quit actin' like the way they
act. What I want to say is that I
hope that everybody makes the right
choices. What I want to say is I
wish people would go to school and stop
skippin' so much. What I want to say.*

22 *Between the Houses,* 1994
Oil on board, 9 x 10 in.

23 *After the Rain,* 1997
Oil on linen, 19 x 20 in.

24 *Looking Back,* 1995
Oil on linen, 44 x 54 in.

25 *Milwaukee's Hope III,* 1994
Oil on linen, 36 x 44 in.

26 *Near Cambridge Avenue,* 1996
Oil on linen, 16 x 29 in.

27 *New Purple Paint,* 1994
Oil on linen, 24 x 24 in.

HOODMOMMAS
REVIVING AFRICAN TRADITIONS OF MOTHERING

By Tanya Cromartie-Twaddle

Mario's plastic shotgun is tucked away in a hole in the wall of my basement. Every now and then, when I'm on my way up the stairs from the laundry room, the orange barrel catches my eye and a tiny tinge of guilt pulls at me. But I am strong and shake it off quick with a maternal smile. I naturally know what is good for him. Two summers ago I snatched this dreadful toy from the sidewalk where it lay during a break from Mario's play. I had chastised him over and over again about the dangers of pointing it at cars and offered him alternatives to his shoot-'em-up and leave-'em-dead games.

Of course, he was hardheaded and wouldn't listen. I confiscated his toy and never told anyone.

My mother instinct assures me it was the right thing to do.

Funny thing is, I am not his mother.

But I am his othermother and take collective responsibility for his upbringing.

I have always been curious about this inherent nerve black women possess, this unspoken permission to parent other people's children. It is a lost art that we must revive for the sake of healing our communities.

I grew up in the south among women, blood related and otherwise who all had a say in my daily life. I had several women to answer to. I was raised with many eyes watching me and a gathering of mother spirits who kept me in the fold when my mother was physically or emotionally absent. This practice strengthened the weak spots in my family life and fostered my connection to the larger community.

I firmly believe that motherhood was never meant to be a private responsibility.

In most African societies, past and present, mothering stretches beyond biology. Black motherhood was once a fluid and ever-accommodating network of shared mothering. Momma was the central warm belly of the village that all would come to for nourishment and comfort. Mother was every woman, and her arms stretched wide enough for everyone, no matter what her circumstances or means.

Unfortunately, we have allowed ourselves to be nearly severed from our greatest salvation.

It is these creatively extended family relationships of othermothers, godmothers, bloodmothers, aunties, grandmas and sisters that have helped the disenfranchised diaspora endure. Community mothering has kept us together. Yet we are not tending to those cultural roots well enough. My mother says it isn't like it used to be. Used to be an unfamiliar child would respect her word. Listen to her telling him right from wrong. These days she's likely to get cussed out. Respect for our elders has diminished greatly among our young sons and daughters. As this aura of community mothering has faded, so has our young people's connection to the community. The lack of community connection makes it impossible for our young people to respect themselves and the rights of others. The mob beatings and culture of youth violence that plagues Milwaukee's inner city is a direct result of this disconnection. The socio-economic stressors that have caused women to distance themselves from collective responsibility, the adoption of Eurocentric models of parenting from over 300 years ago and this need, born from fear and desperation, to save ourselves – all have crippled our ability to heal Milwaukee's 'hoods as fast as we need to. We have accepted parenting as a private burden and too often leave it up to social service agencies to help us raise our children.

Academics black and white alike have studied parenting from myriad angles. Scholars have made unprecedented strides and have debunked many of our old-school rules of parenting. They have the nerve to assert that our ancestors, parents and grandparents raised children on simple adages. I disagree. The respect for native folk wisdom and natural simplicity is what we need more of. The old African proverb is wisdom for a reason. It does take a village to raise a child. We don't need more jails, social service institutions and graves to hold our sons and daughters. Families have to band together and take our children back from the streets. We must call our mothers in from the fringes of the village and restore our ancient ways of doing this sacred motherwork. We need more healthy, supported and empowered bloodmothers, othermothers, hoodmommas tending to this difficult work of community healing in Milwaukee.

And I will never give my neighbor's son back his plastic shotgun.

28 *Two Tone*, 1997
Oil on board, 11 1/4 x 15 in.

29 *Two Girls,* 1997
Oil on linen, 24 x 26 in.

30 *Cold Day,* 1993
Oil on linen, 23 x 25 in.

HOW THE BOYS & GIRLS CLUB SAVED MY LIFE

By Coretta Herring

Milwaukee's Hillside Housing Project in the 1970s was the worst place for any young child to grow up – until the summer of 1977. Gang activity, alcohol abuse, drugs, violence and negative peer pressure were everyday realities.

When some new construction started right in the middle of the housing projects, the word was out that it was going to be a police station. That would have helped the neighborhood in those rough days, but what it turned out to be helped even more: the Hillside Boys & Girls Club.

I could hardly wait for the club to be built. The soon-to-be director, Mr. John Williams, would often show up at the construction site and tell all the kids that the building was going to be a safe and fun place to come to.

31 *Harp Lights (A view of Wisconsin Avenue),* 1999
Watercolor on paper, 9 x 11 1/2 in.

I remember counting down the days with my sister. We made sure we were the first in line when the door opened. I still remember my club card number. It was 1mg, which stood for first midget girl. When the club opened, my life changed forever. I was captivated by the staff's warmth and personality. The club allowed me to participate in basketball, soccer, track and field, volleyball, the Torchette Club (a community service club for young girls) and the Keystone Club, teaching leadership to teens. My grades in school improved drastically. The very first time I traveled outside of Milwaukee I went with the club to Washington, D.C., for a Keystone Conference. My single mother did the best she could as a low-income parent. She became a full-time volunteer and continued to be until her death in 2000. The club allowed my family to explore life to the fullest by eliminating the barriers that separated us from accomplishing our professional and economic aspirations.

I received my first job through the clubs, and they supported me through college, where I obtained my associate degree in administrative assistance. After graduation I pursued my career working for St. Joseph's Hospital for five years. I never left the clubs; I became a faithful volunteer all five years. I had to stay close because I was waiting for my dream job to open. It seemed like the office manager would not leave! Finally I got word that a new club was being built, and I placed my bid and became a winner!

Today I am a full-time student at Upper Iowa University, where I will soon receive a bachelor's degree in human services. My career with the clubs spans 25 years – 11 years as a member, nine years as a staff member and five years as a volunteer. I now serve as a full time office manager and I volunteer countless hours as Keystone Club adviser at the Roger and Leona Fitzsimonds Boys & Girls Club.

My future plans are to continue giving the clubs what they gave me as a child!

32 *Morning Sun (Junior Achievement)*, 1998
Oil on linen, 20 x 29 in.

33 *My Neighborhood
(Hand-me-down),* 1998
Oil on linen, 22 x 23 in.

34 *Hooded Boy,* 1998
Oil on linen, 19 x 20 in.

35 *Moon Halo,* 2004
Oil on linen, 15 x 16 in.

ON CHARACTER-BASED EDUCATION

By Richard R. Pieper Sr.

We are born equal. This is what we believe, in a nation that works overtime to ensure free and equal access to all. One could make a case that we are democracy crazy. We go to extraordinary means to allow freedom and opportunity for everyone. In practice, though, there remain important questions: Does everyone have the same chromosomes, peers, family, neighbors, friends, people who care and love them? Obviously, no. Does everyone in economic poverty stay there? Many people are able to move out of poverty. More important, possibly, is spiritual and emotional poverty. Here we have only evolving knowledge.

Our social service agencies, war machine, diplomacy and the United Nations spend enormous efforts on resources to correct bad decisions, yet we blunder a lot in our efforts, and the entire process brings questionable results.

Everything will never be as our Maker has wished for us. (We can question if there is a watchmaker for the watch.) I believe we have the possibility of leading celestial lives, but for almost all of us – if we are so fortunate – only at moments can our journey touch perfection. Still, our examples of serving and living for the correct reasons say much to others. Teaching basic virtues, seeking understanding of them, then acting them out early in life may be more effective than treating the symptoms of human tragedy. (Examples: Learning for Life, Character Education Partnership, Boy Scouts of America.)

"To educate a man in mind and not in morals is to educate a menace to society." —President Theodore Roosevelt.

"Intelligence is not enough. Intelligence plus character – that is the goal of true education."—Rev. Martin Luther King Jr.

"The leader always knows what (the goal) is and can articulate it for any who are unsure."—Robert K. Greenleaf on Servant Leadership.

David's work represents all of this. His city scenes are representative of community and its evolving citizens. His farm scenes represent a class of working people who have spent their lives engaged in rich, meaningful work. Their work is filled with virtue and character that tugs at your soul. Hope, character and virtue are beautifully woven throughout his paintings.

What could one hope for in life that is richer than respect, dignity and hope (in the city scenes) or to have spent your gift of life in meaningful work (in the farm scenes)? David's capturing of such a rich fabric of living and his example of serving say much to all of us.

36 *Learning For Life Field Days,* 2001
Oil on linen, 18 x 24 in.

37 *Lone Tree,* 2004
Oil on linen, 14 x 14 in.

38 *The Familiar Path*, 2004
Oil on linen, 28 x 34 in.

PAINTING THE WAGNERS

By Crocker Stephenson

David is painting their faces, Erv and Mercedes' ancient, aging faces.

It's something of a departure. For most of his career, David has painted children. Usually, they are children at play in the city, in Milwaukee. A child about to sled down Reservoir Hill. A child climbing on rocks near the inner harbor. Two kids strolling down Wisconsin Ave.

The paintings are highly detailed and powerfully realistic. The best have a bright and fleeting innocence about them that viewers find moving. When adults look at the paintings, they see familiar houses, office buildings and factories. They see children at play in the city where they work. And the children, painted with David's luminous, atmospheric palette, are bathed in light. The children are haunting.

David was a different man when he started painting children. He was a young man, himself at play in an occupation that he had dreamed of since he was a child. He is no longer a young man. He is 38. He is a husband. A father. His love for Rosemarie and Sam rivets him, bolts him, to the spinning world.

Such connectedness takes its toll.

"No Fear" is a popular mantra. You see it on T-shirts and on bumper stickers plastered to the rear ends of mud-spattered trucks. But only the uncommitted can afford to be fearless. Those whose hearts are attached to the world know the kind of fear that only love can muster. They know that there is a difference between fearlessness and courage.

That is what David admires about the Wagners: their courage, measured by the depth of their commitment. Painting their portrait enlarges him; it is a meditation on courage.

And so David paints their faces. And he paints the light so that it strikes them from behind, igniting the fuzz on the tips of Erv's ears, blasting through their clothes, creating a halo out of Mercedes' hair.

"We will have been married fifty years this February tenth," Mercedes says. "It's hard to believe all the years that have gone by. All the changes in life."

The Wagners were milking 15 cows the year they got married, which was then the state average. The Wagners are still milking 15 cows, though the state average has grown to 66. They know they've fallen behind the times. Erv, who sometimes describes himself as "an old-time farmer," shrugs.

"We're still in business," he says. "We're not making no money, but hell, look: We're still here."

Their survival is a point of pride. In nominal dollars, the average annual price farmers got for milk hit historic highs in 1996. But adjusted for inflation, milk prices peaked in 1979 and have been in decline ever since. They are now roughly 80% of their 1960 value. In other words, the milk the Wagners produce is worth four-fifths of what it was 40 years ago. And look: They're still here.

"That's the way it is," Mercedes says. "We've had hard times. We've had poor times. You're going to hit a lot of bumps in the road before you're done. I don't care what you do. No matter what you have. Might as well take the bumps. It's not all peaches and pretty.

"You get married for better or worse, and sometimes there was worse before better came around. But we're here."

Erv points to the wall of the barn. Initials have been scratched into the soft stone.

" 'HW,' that's my dad's name. The 'H' goes for Henry. Henry Wagner. 'MW,' that's my sister, Muriel, Muriel Wagner. Here's my brother, Albert Wagner. See there. 'EW.' Erv Wagner. I was probably 12 years old when we carved those in. I can remember putting them in there. Did it with a jackknife.

"Now this one here – 'RJ' – I don't know who that would be. I don't think I know any 'RJ.' Probably was a movie star who came by here." Erv laughs. "Movie stars are always stopping in."

In the painting, it is morning. Erv and Mercedes have finished milking. They have walked down their driveway a ways and have stopped. It is autumn. The thistle has gone to seed. The seed is scattered in the grass at their feet.

David Lenz had set out to paint a portrait of his friends, dairy farmers Erv and Mercedes Wagner. And while it may seem as if his young, urban, somewhat etiolated middle-class life has little in common with their elderly, rural, sunburned world, it is extraordinary, David feels, how deeply he and they contain each other, and he is moved to discover that this portrait of Erv and Mercedes Wagner is a portrait not only of the Wagners' marriage, but also of his own.

David places the sun out of frame but still low in the sky; its incumbent light is piercing.

An excerpt from the series Canvas & Plow, *published February 4, 2001 in the Milwaukee Journal Sentinel.*
©2004 Journal Sentinel Inc., reproduced with permission.

39 *Thistles,* 2001
Oil on linen, 32 x 54 in.

40 *The Sick Cow,* 2002
Oil on board, 11 x 9 ¹/₄ in.

41 *Getting in the Cows,* 2001
Oil on linen, 17 x 19 in.

PRESERVING WISCONSIN'S FARMLAND

By Rod Nilsestuen,

Wisconsin Secretary of Agriculture, Trade and Consumer Protection

Having grown up in Trempealeau County, I know something about conservation. On those steep hillsides, you learn pretty quickly that if you don't take care of the land it won't take care of you.

In his classic book *The Land Remembers*, Ben Logan explains this connection to the land so many of us feel:

Once you have lived on the land, been a partner with its moods, secrets, and seasons, you cannot leave. The living land remembers, touching you in unguarded moments, saying, "I am here. You are part of me."

Logan, who grew up in rural Wisconsin, captures what most of us who value farming feel … an almost spiritual connection to the land … a connection to the soil that nurtures us … to the red barns of memory … to the farm life of our youth.

That connection is both our strength and our Achilles heel. That connection gives us roots and reminds us that what we do is important. Sometimes, it also blinds us to external forces … whether to the economic reality of our declining competitiveness in the dairy industry … or to the mounting pressure to address how we site large animal operations and other rural development projects … or to the incredibly rapid conversion of farmland to strip malls and subdivisions.

Farmland and Future Generations

Wisconsin can and should be recognized for its environmentally friendly land use. The state's farmers provide habitat for wildlife, and with proper soil conservation and nutrient management can maintain groundwater and surface-water quality as well as quantity. As Wisconsin grows, agriculture based on proven conservation practices may be the best insurance we have to leave a sound environmental legacy to future generations.

In 1950 there were 24 million acres of farmland in Wisconsin. Today, there are about 16 million acres, down by a third. The National Resource Inventory indicates 152,100 acres of farmland were converted to urban use in the 1980s, while nearly that same amount was converted in just the first five years of the 1990s! The triangle between Madison, Milwaukee and Chicago is the third highest in the entire nation in terms of farmland conversion.

Farmland Preservation – Time for A New Look

Land use management is a local matter in Wisconsin. Although we have the Farmland Preservation Program, the program is only as good as local government can make it. Effective farmland preservation hinges on maintaining a dynamic and comprehensive land use plan developed with broad-based community input and buy-in while accounting for current land-use patterns and trends.

In the past 20 years, the number of Wisconsin farms has decreased 18%, and acres in farms decreased 13%. Despite these significant changes, just two counties have developed new agricultural preservation plans during that period. One of these – Jefferson County – reports the conversion of farmland to urban uses declined by an amazing 90% in the first year after they implemented a well-designed new plan. This proves that with political will, with real commitment and with active involvement of the whole community, it can be done. Our farmland can be saved for future generations.

An Opportunity Right Now

We have an opportunity right now to rethink how we approach farmland preservation. We need to adopt an integrated approach, planning not only for farmland preservation but also conservation and agricultural growth. And we need to involve everyone in this planning, from state officials to county and town planners, to the farmers who know and live on the land that means so much to us all. Our state's culture and economy is deeply rooted in the long and proud traditions of people working in partnership with the land. That connection must continue or we will all be diminished. Subdivisions will never again become farms.

We have a window of opportunity. There is growing consensus that action is needed. The next generation is depending on us.

42 *Dairyland,* 2003
Oil on linen, 30 x 36 in.

THE LAND REMEMBERS

By Ben Logan

Once you have lived on the land, been a partner with its moods, secrets, and seasons, you cannot leave. The living land remembers, touching you in unguarded moments, saying, "I am here. You are part of me."

When this happens to me, I go home again, in mind or in person, back to a hilltop world in southwestern Wisconsin.... That land is my genesis. I was born there, cradled by the land, and I am always there even though I have been a wanderer.

I cannot leave the land. How can I when a thousand sounds, sights, and smells tell me I am part of it? Let me hear the murmur of talk in the dusk of a summer night and I am sitting again under the big maple tree in the front yard, hearing the voices of people I have loved. Mother listens to the whippoorwills with that look the sound always brings to her face. Father has just come from the oat field across the dusty road. He sits with a half dozen stems in his hands, running his fingers along the heads of grain, asking the oats if tomorrow is the day harvest should begin.

Let me hear drying plants rattle somewhere in a cold wind and I am with the corn-shredding crew. Men are talking about the hill country. "Why, my father used to say he dropped a milk pail once. By the time it stop rolling, couple days later, it was all the way down in the valley. Fellow who lived there said he hadn't bought a new milk pail in thirty years. Didn't know where they came from, he said, they just rolled in any time he needed one."

There is laughter. A big man slaps his thigh.

"Never happens to me," says another voice. "I got me some square milk pails."

Let me feel the softness of ground carpeted with pine needles and I am lying on my back in the middle of a great grove of trees, looking up to where the swaying tops touch the blue. Around me are my three brothers, and we argue endlessly about the mystery of the pines. Where did they come from? How old are they? Could a tree that's three feet through and eighty feet tall come from a seed not much bigger than the head of a pin?

Let the smell of mint touch me. I am kneeling along a little stream, the water numbing my hands as I reach for a trout. I feel the fish arch and struggle. I let go, pulling watercress from the water instead.

Let me see a certain color and I am standing beside the threshing machine, grain cascading through my hands. The seeds we planted when snow was spitting down have multiplied a hundred times, returning in a stream of bright gold, still warm with the sunlight of the fields.

Let me hear an odd whirring. I am deep in the woods, following an elusive sound, looking in vain for a last passenger pigeon, a feathered lightning I have never seen, unwilling to believe no person will ever see one again.

Let me look from a window to see sunlight glitter on a winding stream and I am in the one-room schoolhouse in Halls Branch Valley. A young teacher has asked me to stay after school because of a question I asked. Voice full of emotion as it seldom is during the school day, she reads to me of an Indian speaking to his people. He sweeps his hands in a circle, taking in all lands, seas, creatures, and plants, all suns, stars, and moons. "We are a People, one tiny fragment in the immense mosaic of life. What are we without the corn, the rabbit, the sun, the rain, and the deer? Know this, my people: The *all* does not belong to us. We belong to the *all*."

Let me hear seasons changing in the night. It is any season and I am every age I have ever been. Streams are wakening in the spring, rain wets the dust of summer, fallen apples ferment in an orchard, snow pelts the frozen land and puts stocking caps of white on the fence posts.

I cannot leave the land.

The land remembers. It says, "I am here. You are part of me."

An excerpt from the book The Land Remembers, *published by NorthWord Press.*
©*1999 by Ben T. Logan*

43 *Erv's Haven,* 2003
Oil on linen, 28 x 48 in.

44 *Massey Ferguson 285,* 2004
Watercolor on paper, 13 x 14 in.

BIOGRAPHY & EXHIBITION HISTORY

Born Milwaukee, Wisconsin 1962.
B.F.A. University of Wisconsin-Milwaukee, 1985.
Web site: www.davidmlenz.com

SELECTED EXHIBITIONS

Leigh Yawkey Woodson Art Museum, Wausau, Wisconsin:
Beyond City Limits: Rural Views of the Midwest, group show, 2004.

Madison Art Center, Madison:
Wisconsin Triennial, jury group show, 2002.

Charles Allis Art Museum, Milwaukee:
Self & Other Portraits: Wisconsin Artists, group show, 2002.

Milwaukee Lakefront, Milwaukee:
Lakefront Festival of Arts, jury group show, 1990 - 1998 and in 2002.
Awards 1990, 1993, 1996, 1998, 2002.

Charles Allis Art Museum, Milwaukee:
Thistles, solo show, 2001.

Purdue University Union Gallery, West Lafayette, Indiana:
Three Realists, group show, 1997.

Madison Art Center, Madison:
Wisconsin Triennial, jury group show, 1993.

West Bend Gallery of Fine Art, West Bend, Wisconsin:
New Work, group show, 1991.

Richard Love Gallery, Chicago:
Rural Scenes, group show, 1989.

SELECTED BIBLIOGRAPHY

Auer, James. *Climbing a Hill: Mural Pays Homage to the Bravery of Children with Illnesses.* Milwaukee Journal Sentinel, September 21, 2000. Article online at: http://www.jsonline.com/enter/finearts/sep00/lenz21092000.asp

Auer, James. *Before the Fireworks: Art Imitates Life to Immortalize a Milwaukee Tradition.* The Milwaukee Journal, July 3, 1994.

Auer, James. *Reproductions of Lenz Painting Reward Contributions to Group.* The Milwaukee Journal, July 29, 1993.

Massey, Jim. *'Thistles' to Hang in DATCP office.* The Country Today, April 21, 2004.

Pabst, Nick. *Through the Eyes of an Artist: City's Good Nature Shines Through in Painter's Realistic Look at its Neighborhoods.* The Milwaukee Journal, July 12, 1990.

Pearson, Jack. *The People's Choice: Local Artist Captures Soul of the City.* Exclusively Yours Magazine, April 1994.

Reed, W.A. *David M. Lenz: Portrait of a Social Realist.* Porcupine Literary Arts Magazine, winter 1997.

Stephenson, Crocker. *Canvas & Plow: A Wisconsin Elegy.* Four-part Sunday series in the Milwaukee Journal Sentinel, January 14 through February 4, 2001. Articles online at: www.jsonline.com/news/farm

Stephenson, Crocker. *Fruitful: Pappa Sendik Portrait Reaps Memories.* Milwaukee Sentinel, June 9, 1991.

Stezenski, Tammy. *Remembering the Family Farm: Why the Latest Exhibit at the Leigh Yawkey Woodson Art Museum is About More than Art.* (Wausau, Wisconsin) City Pages, July 15-22, 2004.

CATALOGUE OF THE EXHIBIT

Note: Height precedes width in all measurements.

1 *Tugboat,* 1998
Oil on board, 11 1/4 x 18 in.
Lent by Mr. and Mrs. Daniel J. Bader

2 *Riverwest,* 1990
Oil on linen, 41 x 53 in.
Lent by Northwestern Mutual Insurance Co.

3 *Batchewaung Bay, Quetico Provincial Park,* 1984
Oil on board, 14 x 11 in.
Lent by the artist

4 *Ballard Lake, Wisconsin,* 1985
Oil on board, 14 x 11 in.
Lent by Mr. and Mrs. Thomas E. Lenz

5 *Bud-Fern Falls, Quetico Provincial Park,* 1984
Oil on board, 11 x 14 in.
Lent by the artist

6 *From Trail Ridge Road, Rocky Mountain National Park,* 1996
Watercolor on paper, 5 3/4 x 8 3/4 in.
Lent by the artist

7 *Sunrise,* 1998
Oil on linen, 20 x 24 in.
Lent by Barbara Stein

8 *Student,* 1993
Oil on board, 9 x 10 in.
Lent by Craig and Lisa Zetley

9 *Looking South,* 2002
Oil on linen, 12 x 18 in.
Lent by John and Lynn Leopold

10 *Portrait of Sam Lenz,* 1999
Oil on board, 6 x 7 in.
Lent by Rosemarie Feiza-Lenz

11 *No Luck Today,* 1995
Oil on linen, 26 x 36 in.
Lent by Nancy Aten and Daniel Collins

12 *North Avenue,* 1990
Oil on linen, 14 1/4 x 20 in.
Lent by Mr. and Mrs. John F. Monroe Jr.

13 *Seated Boy,* 1992
Oil on board, 9 x 10 in.
Lent by Steve and Jane Chernof

14 *New Faces,* 1992
Oil on board, 9 x 10 in.
Lent by Patricia Goldreich

15 *Newhall Street,* 1992
Oil on linen, 26 x 32 in.
Lent by West Bend Mutual Insurance Co.

16 *The Black Door,* 1993
Oil on board, 9 x 10 in.
Lent by Sally S. Stevens

17 *Hang Tough,* 1991
Oil on linen, 36 x 42 1/2 in.
Lent by Mr. and Mrs. Daniel J. Bader

18 *Before the Fireworks,* 1993
Oil on linen, 66 x 144 in.
Lent by Barbara Stein

19 *Milwaukee's Hope,* 1992
Oil on linen, 40 x 54 in.
Lent by Martin F. Stein

20 *Peace in Our Neighborhood,* 1993
Oil on linen, 19 x 22 in.
Lent by Martin F. Stein

21 *Snowy Day,* 1993
Oil on linen, 20 x 22 in.
Lent by a private collection

22 *Between the Houses,* 1994
Oil on board, 9 x 10 in.
Lent by Phyllis Hoyer

23 *After the Rain,* 1997
Oil on linen, 19 x 20 in.
Lent by Mr. and Mrs. Leslie Muma

24 *Looking Back,* 1995
Oil on linen, 44 x 54 in.
Lent by Mr. and Mrs. Daniel J. Bader

25 *Milwaukee's Hope III,* 1994
Oil on linen, 36 x 44 in.
Lent by Mr. and Mrs. Leslie Muma

26 *Near Cambridge Avenue,* 1996
Oil on linen, 16 x 29 in.
Lent by John and Lynn Leopold

27 *New Purple Paint,* 1994
Oil on linen, 24 x 24 in.
Lent by Mr. and Mrs. Richard R. Pieper Sr.

28 *Two Tone,* 1997
Oil on board, 11 1/4 x 15 in.
Lent by Dr. and Mrs. Paul Goldstein

29 *Two Girls,* 1997
Oil on linen, 24 x 26 in.
Lent by Steve and Jane Chernof

30 *Cold Day,* 1993
Oil on linen, 23 x 25 in.
Lent by a private collection

31 *Harp Lights (A view of Wisconsin Avenue),* 1999
Watercolor on paper, 9 x 11 1/2 in.
Lent by Mr. and Mrs. George Dalton

32 *Morning Sun (Junior Achievement),* 1998
Oil on linen, 20 x 29 in.
Lent by Ned and Helen Bechthold

33 *My Neighborhood (Hand-me-down),* 1998
Oil on linen, 22 x 23 in.
Lent by Mr. and Mrs. Thomas R. Tuschen

34 *Hooded Boy,* 1998
Oil on linen, 19 x 20 in.
Lent by Dr. and Mrs. Donald Whitlock

35 *Moon Halo,* 2004
Oil on linen, 15 x 16 in.
Lent by the artist

36 *Learning For Life Field Days,* 2001
Oil on linen, 18 x 24 in.
Lent by Boy Scouts of America – Milwaukee County Council

37 *Lone Tree,* 2004
Oil on linen, 14 x 14 in.
Lent by the artist

38 *The Familiar Path,* 2004
Oil on linen, 28 x 34 in.
Lent by the artist

39 *Thistles,* 2001
Oil on linen, 32 x 54 in.
Lent by Pieper Electric Inc.

40 *The Sick Cow,* 2002
Oil on board, 11 x 9 1/4 in.
Lent by Mr. and Mrs. Dennis Wallestad

41 *Getting in the Cows,* 2001
Oil on linen, 17 x 19 in.
Lent by Mr. and Mrs. John F. Monroe Jr.

42 *Dairyland,* 2003
Oil on linen, 30 x 36 in.
Lent by the artist

43 *Erv's Haven,* 2003
Oil on linen, 28 x 48 in.
Lent by the artist

44 *Massey Ferguson 285,* 2004
Watercolor on paper, 13 x 14 in.
Lent by the artist

43 *Erv's Haven (Detail),* 2003
Oil on linen, 28 x 48 in.

Daniel J. Bader
Diverse Milwaukee

Mr. Bader is the current chairman of the Greater Milwaukee Committee, a civic organization made up of the region's corporate, nonprofit and educational leaders. He is president of the third largest foundation in the city, the Helen Bader Foundation. Since 1992, the foundation has made more than $124 million in grants and facilitated idea sharing in support of a range of charitable efforts, primarily in Wisconsin and Israel. Mr. Bader is devoted to using the foundation's intellectual and financial resources to best serve people in need. He resides on Milwaukee's east side with his wife, Linda, and their three children.

Tiara Cannon, Marlisa Harris and Carlton Young
Three poems

Ms. Cannon, Ms. Harris and Mr. Young were students in the summer 2004 Poetry Camp at Woodland Pattern Book Center, 720 E. Locust Street. Ms. Cannon is an eighth-grader at the Milwaukee Education Center who loves to draw and sings in her church choir. Ms. Harris is a sophomore at James Madison University High School who enjoys writing poetry and playing basketball, and wants to study law. Mr. Young is an eighth-grader at the Wisconsin Conservatory of Lifelong Learning in Milwaukee. He enjoys math, reading, drawing, swimming and ice-skating, and would like to be an architect.

Tanya Cromartie-Twaddle
Hoodmommas: Reviving African Traditions of Mothering

Ms. Cromartie-Twaddle is first and foremost the mother of two girls. She is Cultural Arts Coordinator for COA Youth & Family Centers and United Neighborhood Centers of Milwaukee. She's a folk artist and poet, and she writes a column about social and race issues for the Riverwest Currents newspaper. She has worked with Milwaukee youth for 10 years through youth centers and community organizing.

Jeffrey R. Hayes
Painting the Unsung: An Interview with David M. Lenz.

Prof. Hayes earned a PhD in art history from the University of Maryland in 1982, and moved in that year to Milwaukee, to join the faculty of the University of Wisconsin-Milwaukee, where he is now professor of art history. His teaching area is American art, and his research focuses on folk and early modern art and contemporary self-taught artists. He also directs UWM's interdisciplinary Master of Liberal Studies program, where he offers an annual seminar on American history, literature and visual culture.

Coretta Herring
How the Boys & Girls Club Saved My Life

Ms. Herring is an alumna of the Hillside Boys & Girls Club and serves as the office manager and teen advisor at the Fitzsimonds Club in Milwaukee's Metcalfe Park. She lives in Milwaukee with her husband and three boys and attends Upper Iowa University, pursuing a bachelor's degree in social work, which she expects to complete in 2005. Her late mother, Jannie Hardnett, is her inspiration.

Ben Logan
The Land Remembers, excerpt

Mr. Logan first published *The Land Remembers* in 1975. It's now in its seventh edition, and has sold approximately 400,000 copies. He spent 20 years working in the media in New York, where he won many awards in film and TV, but has returned to the southwestern Wisconsin farm of his childhood. "You can go home again," he says, "just so you don't try to be who you were when you left." His other books include a novel, *The Empty Meadow,* and a memoir, *Christmas Remembered.*

Rod Nilsestuen
Preserving Wisconsin's Farmland

Mr. Nilsestuen is secretary of the Wisconsin Department of Agriculture, Trade and Consumer Protection. He grew up on a dairy farm in west-central Wisconsin, one of seven children. His brothers still farm. He has a bachelor's degree in political science from UW-River Falls and a UW law degree. For two decades he led the Wisconsin Federation of Cooperatives; he was inducted last year into the national Cooperative Hall of Fame. He lives in DeForest with his wife, Carol. They have three grown sons.

Richard R. Pieper Sr.
On Character-Based Education

Mr. Pieper is Chairman and CEO of PPC Partners Inc., parent company of Pieper Electric Co., a top U.S. electrical contracting firm. He is a board member of Junior Achievement, Boy Scouts of America, Learning for Life, and Boys & Girls Clubs, among other organizations, and is a former 12-year board member of the Milwaukee Art Museum. He has trained many non-profit executives in outcomes management and collaboration and has endowed university and college chairs in Servant Leadership.

Martin F. Stein
Healing the World: The American Tradition of Doing Good

Mr. Stein is the founder of the Stein Drugs and Stein Optical chains of stores. He is a legendary philanthropist, and a member of numerous local, national and international boards. He has held board leadership positions in the Boys & Girls Clubs, Junior Achievement, Big Brothers Big Sisters and the United Jewish Appeal. He has chaired capital campaigns for the Betty Brinn Children's Museum, America's Black Holocaust Museum and Operation Moses, which rescued Ethiopian Jews and brought them to Israel. He is the proud father of two grown sons and the grandfather of three granddaughters.

Crocker Stephenson
Painting the Wagners, excerpt from Canvas & Plow

Mr. Stephenson has been writing for the Milwaukee Sentinel and the Milwaukee Journal Sentinel for 17 years. His stories have won many local, state and national awards. Currently one of the Journal Sentinel's local columnists, he was on the paper's Special Projects Team when he wrote *Canvas & Plow,* a series of feature articles about David Lenz's work with Erv and Mercedes Wagner. Mr. Stephenson lives in Shorewood with his three children.